WHAT MAKES A HERO?
LEADER GUIDE

What Makes a Hero?
The Death-Defying Ministry of Jesus

What Makes a Hero?
978-1-5018-4792-9
978-1-5018-4793-6 eBook

What Makes a Hero? DVD
978-1-5018-4796-7

What Makes a Hero? Youth Study Book
978-1-5018-4803-2
978-1-5018-4804-9 eBook

What Makes a Hero? Children's Leader Guide
978-1-5018-4791-2

What Makes a Hero? Worship Resources Flash Drive
978-1-5018-4805-6

Also by Matt Rawle

The Faith of a Mockingbird
Hollywood Jesus
The Salvation of Doctor Who
The Redemption of Scrooge

MATT RAWLE

WHAT MAKES A
HERO?
THE DEATH-DEFYING
MINISTRY OF JESUS

LEADER GUIDE BY BEN SIMPSON

Abingdon Press / Nashville

What Makes a Hero?
The Death-Defying Ministry of Jesus
Leader Guide

This book is printed on elemental chlorine-free paper.
978-1-5018-4794-3

17 18 19 20 21 22 23 24 25 26 — 10 9 8 7 6 5 4 3 2 1
MANUFACTURED IN THE UNITED STATES OF AMERICA

CONTENTS

A NOTE TO GROUP LEADERS

Hero stories are hot. DC Comics and Marvel have both had tremendous success translating popular comic book stories to the silver screen. These films are filled with compelling characters and fast-paced action. We cheer the protagonists and jeer the villains. It is also interesting to see how multiple storylines converge as part of a cinematic universe. DC Comics and Marvel aren't just telling good stories, they are inviting us into another world.

When Jesus came among us announcing the kingdom of God, he proclaimed that another world was possible. But the Kingdom he announced was not just the product of his imagination. It was a reality he came to enact and embody. In seeing Jesus, we see the Kingdom. And by becoming his followers, we participate in his resurrection work as he makes all things new, including us.

In *What Makes a Hero? The Death-Defying Ministry of Jesus*, Matt Rawle invites us to see that our present fascination with hero stories points beyond those stories to the person and work of Jesus Christ. The good news about Jesus challenges and transcends the great themes found in each of these stories in awesome and powerful ways. Rawle invites us to see beyond pop culture and into the gospel to discover the life God has for us.

As a group leader, your role is to facilitate weekly sessions using the book *What Makes a Hero?* as well as this Leader Guide, and the accompanying DVD. This guide includes instructions on how to structure a sixty-minute session. Each session opens with a lesson aim, a few themes to develop, a primary selection from the Bible, and a quotation from the author that identifies a major theological theme. Then, there are three major movements for each session:

1. Connecting Communally with the Topic;
2. Taking a Closer Look: Video, Book, and Scripture; and
3. Sending Forth: Equipped to Serve the World.

The first and last sections should take about ten minutes each, while the second section should receive the majority of your focus as you discuss the video, book, and a passage from Scripture.

Make sure to read through each session prior to your gathering. Consider your words carefully, and if you know the participants, prayerfully consider what points of discussion will be most helpful for them. The goal is to help each person take a next step with Jesus Christ. This Leader Guide contains plenty of breadth, so you will need to be selective if you wish to go deep on one or two discussion questions or if you think it would be best to spend an extended period of time engaged with the Scripture. Come to each session prayerfully prepared.

By leading this study you are being faithful to Jesus' command to teach and disciple others. In a way, you are being a hero, all because Jesus has been a hero to you. Lives can be changed in this study. Salvation can be experienced. God is enfolding your group into *his* story. Pay attention as God is at work. Put what you learn into action. God is always faithful. Respond to God with faith.

Session One
GOOD, EVIL, AND GOD

SESSION OVERVIEW

Lesson Aim

To differentiate between good and evil by drawing upon Scripture, reason, tradition, and experience and to choose what is good by imitating Jesus.

Session Themes

- To examine pop culture examples that resonate with our longing to see good triumph over evil.
- To explore those longings theologically in light of Christian claims about God.
- To recognize and understand the difference between good and evil.
- To commit to acts of justice and grow in fellowship with God by following Jesus in daily life.

- To grow in confidence that good will win out in the end.
- To live today in light of that confidence.

Hero Focus: Batman

In each chapter, Matt Rawle cites multiple hero stories to illustrate important biblical and theological concepts. In this chapter, you may want to focus your group on the example of Batman when exploring good and evil. Batman first appeared in 1939 in *Detective Comics* #2 and was created by Bob Kane and Bill Finger. Batman is the secret identity of Bruce Wayne, a wealthy American playboy, philanthropist, and owner of Wayne Enterprises. Batman does not possess supernatural abilities, but rather utilizes stealth, combat training, a keen intellect, and technological wizardry to thwart crime. His most notable enemies include Joker, Riddler, Two-Face, Catwoman, and Poison Ivy. Visit Wikipedia on the Internet and read the entry for Batman if you would like more information prior to your gathering.

Key Scripture

Be imitators of God, as beloved children, and live in love as Christ loved us and gave himself up for us.
Ephesians 5:1-2

Theological Focus

Jesus' story is both familiar and completely separate from us. His life, suffering, death, and resurrection mirror our own hero stories in many ways, but Jesus' story is much different. Jesus is the Messiah. It's not that Jesus is better, or stronger, or quicker, or wittier than the rest of us. Jesus *is* us, and at the same time he is altogether different. When we look to Jesus' story we find a common thread, but we also find that the thread is woven into a subversive,

10

upside-down revelation of God's kingdom. Jesus is a new kind of hero.

(Rawle, page 20)

CONNECTING COMMUNALLY WITH THE TOPIC (10 MINUTES)

Welcome the group to the study. Introduce yourself and learn the names of all group participants if you do not already know everyone. Allow time for group members to become acquainted.

In the first session, provide a basic overview of the book resource and the primary themes found within. Share with the group that each session will include discussion, prayer, a video where you will hear from Matt Rawle, a closer look at the book, and an examination of Scripture in light of the theme. Tell the group that you will also look for ways to apply what you have learned and to challenge one another to live in light of the good news revealed in Jesus.

Opening Prayer

God Almighty, you are good. The world you have created is good. Help us today to learn how better to discern good from evil and to commit ourselves to justice, mercy, and walking humbly with you. Amen.

Conversation Starter

Say:

The first chapter in our book explores good, evil, and God. Good and evil are thematically important in many superhero stories, like Batman. How do we discern the difference between good and evil? Where is God at work when we face trial and hardship? How does Jesus invite us into a life with God where we are empowered to do justice, love mercy, and walk humbly with God? In our world discerning good from evil is not always easy, and choosing what is good can be very difficult. Today we will discuss how following Jesus helps us align ourselves with God's work in the world.

Ask and Discuss:

- What are some of your favorite television shows, movies, or other artistic works that illustrate the struggle between good and evil? Contemporary and classical examples will help this discussion. How do these stories or works of art frame our imaginations regarding good and evil?
- How does your faith inform your understanding of good and evil? How does following Jesus help us choose good and work to overcome evil?

TAKING A CLOSER LOOK: VIDEO, BOOK, AND SCRIPTURE (40 MINUTES)

Note: This section allows approximately thirty minutes for discussion of the book and Scripture after the video portion concludes. You will not have time to address every discussion question. Select questions in advance you believe will be most helpful for your group and address those questions first. It may help to put a check mark by the questions you want to cover. If time allows, incorporate additional questions.

The Video

Say:

We will continue our time together with a video featuring Matt Rawle. Rawle will talk about the primary themes of our session today: good, evil, and God. Notice how he explains these themes using pop culture. Make connections to what we have read together in his book. Then, we will discuss both the video and our book together.

Play:

Session One: Good, Evil, and God (running time is approximately 10 minutes)

Say:

Let's keep what Rawle has said in mind as we take a look at the book and examine these themes in light of our calling to live as disciples of Jesus.

The Book

Chapter one explores the prevalent theme of good and evil that is found in all our great hero stories. Rawle invites us to reflect on our longing for what is good and our rejection of evil as a sign that there is a good God working to overcome evil. Rawle also encourages us to reflect on the example of Jesus. In Jesus, goodness has entered the world, and through Jesus God has overcome evil. In response to Jesus, Rawle calls us to trust in him and follow the threefold journey of Micah 6:8, to do justice, love mercy, and walk humbly with God.

Discuss:

- Rawle writes, "The hero is a picture of who we are and what we can never be, and this is why we need them." How do our heroes connect with us, inspire us, and also humble us in our pursuit of doing good?
- Rawle writes that the story of Jesus includes a separation from the familiar when he leaves the realm of heaven and takes on flesh. The author also notes that this puts Jesus into situations of temptation, trial, and suffering. How does the incarnation of God in the person of Jesus help us relate to God?
- How does Jesus' example instruct us in following after him as his disciple? How do we imitate Jesus?

13

- How do we learn to discern good from evil? How do Scripture, reason, tradition, and experience help us reflect theologically on the will of God?
- Rawle writes, "Sometimes when we think about what is good, we think about the feeling something produces or how well something worked." Rawle then argues that sometimes the good involves uncomfortable or unsettling emotions and that results can at times be deceiving. How does faith help us do hard things that are in alignment with God's will, even when doing good is difficult?
- Rawle states, "Not everything we experience is from God." Do you agree with this statement? Why or why not?
- In the section "Evil and Nothingness," Rawle reflects on the story of Job. What does the story of Job teach us with regard to God's way of working to overcome grief, loss, and pain?
- Rawle draws our attention to Micah 6:8, which tells us to do justice, love mercy, and walk humbly with God. Give examples of doing justice, mercy, and learning to walk in humility that you see in your congregation and broader community. How are you participating in those efforts to do good?
- Rawle asks, "What are some of the ways you can walk with God every day?" Share your commitments and ideas with those in your group.
- Rawle writes, "The good news is that God invites us into eternal relationship through Christ, empowered by the Holy Spirit." How does this hope help us face evil and work toward what is good?

The Scripture

In Advance: Use a commentary or Bible dictionary to help you prepare to discuss the Scripture. Become familiar with the text. Add questions for discussion that emerge from your study in addition to those below.

14

Read Aloud: Ephesians 5:1-20

Discuss:

- Ephesians 5:1-2 tells us to "be imitators of God" and to "live in love, as Christ loved us and gave himself up for us." What does it mean to be an imitator of God?
- Ephesians 5:3-7 lists several behaviors that must be rejected by those choosing to live as imitators of God. Reflect on this list theologically. How does this exhortation help us avoid evil? How do we remain humble even while rejecting a way of life that could inflict harm on ourselves and others?
- Ephesians 5:8-14 offers a distinction between walking in light and darkness. What does it mean to walk as children of light? Ephesians 5:14 says, "'Sleeper, awake! / Rise from the dead, / and Christ will shine on you.'" How does trusting Jesus lead to waking and resurrection?
- Ephesians 5:15-16 says we should live "not as unwise people but as wise, making the most of the time." How do we live according to wisdom? What does it mean to make the most of our days?

Conclude by reading Ephesians 5:1-2 one more time. Explain that following Jesus should result in our becoming like him. Jesus displayed the love of God in his words and his actions. We are called to imitate Christ.

Life Application

Say:

Differentiating between good and evil is not always easy, and consistently choosing what is good as a follower of Jesus is both a great challenge and a great invitation of discipleship. In Romans 12:9 Paul writes, "Let love be genuine; hate what is evil, hold fast to what is good." While the heroes in our favorite stories easily discern good from evil, for many of us this is an ongoing learning process.

15

Pass out a piece of paper and a writing utensil to each person in your study. Ask them to make two columns, numbering each one through five. Ask each person to list five good actions they could do in the next week, and five opportunities for doing evil that they may face (gossip, slander, libel, inflating numbers in business, emotional manipulation in sales). Then, ask the class to share what actions they have identified. Ask the group to reflect on how and where they learned which of these actions were good and beneficial and which were evil and harmful. Invite them to cite sources of instruction, whether scriptural, experiential, or from another source of ethical or moral reflection.

Rawle clearly identifies Micah 6:8 as a guidepost for pursuing what is good: doing justice, loving mercy, and walking humbly with God. Ask the class where their ideas for doing good align with one of these three concepts. Then, challenge the class to circle *one good thing* they will commit to doing as a disciple of Jesus in the following week and *one evil thing* they will actively avoid to honor God in the following week.

SENDING FORTH: EQUIPPED TO SERVE THE WORLD (10 MINUTES)

A Final Thought

Say:

God is good. If we are to be "imitators of God," we must consistently choose what is good. We must also undergo transformation as a disciple of Jesus, who will help us as we trust him by changing our hearts so that we will not only *do* good, but *become* good as the Holy Spirit renovates us from the inside out. As a community and as friends who are following Jesus, let's help one another discern good from evil, hold one another accountable, pray for one another, and partner together to bring glory and honor to God by doing justice, loving mercy, and walking humbly with God.

Closing Prayer

Lord Jesus, you are the ultimate hero. You came and walked among us, doing justice, loving mercy, and walking humbly with God. You are our example. You are also our Messiah and Savior. Help us to trust in you and to follow you. Teach us to walk according to your way. Send the Holy Spirit. Fill us, empower us, and embolden us, leading us to do the will of God, embracing good and rejecting evil. Amen.

Session Two
RIGHT, WRONG, AND HOLY

SESSION OVERVIEW

Lesson Aim

To recognize right and wrong as valid but complex categories and to pursue holiness in the way of Jesus Christ.

Session Themes

- To examine the categories of right and wrong.
- To explore the complexity of ethical decision-making.
- To consider pop culture examples that illustrate how difficulties arise in the quest to do right. To contemplate biblical and theological understandings of Satan or the devil.
- To engage with biblical examples that push us beyond simple rule-keeping and into a life of holiness.

- To craft a vision for holiness that involves a reorientation of the heart resulting from faith in Jesus.

Hero Focus: Spider-Man

In each chapter, Matt Rawle cites multiple hero stories to illustrate important biblical and theological concepts. In this chapter, you may want to focus your group on the example of Spider-Man when exploring right and wrong. Spider-Man first appeared in 1962 in *Amazing Fantasy* #15 and was created by Stan Lee and Steve Ditko. Spider-Man is the secret identity of Peter Parker, a very intelligent teenage boy raised by his Aunt May, a widow living in a modest home in New York City. Spider-Man received his special abilities—which includes enhanced strength, agility, ability to cling to most surfaces, and precognition of nearby threats ("spider sense")—after he was bitten by a radioactive spider. His most notable enemies include the Green Goblin, Hobgoblin, Venom, Doctor Octopus, Sandman, and Shocker. Visit Wikipedia on the Internet and read the entry for Spider-Man if you would like more information prior to your gathering.

Key Scripture

"Which of these three, do you think, was a neighbor to the man who fell into the hands of the robbers?" He said, "The one who showed him mercy." Jesus said to him, "Go and do likewise."
Luke 10:36-37

Theological Focus

Following Christ is not about being right or wrong; it's about continuing God's story through holiness of living. Holiness is our calling as Christians.... The gospel calls us to an even higher calling than discerning right from wrong.

We are called to do that which is holy, so that the eternal life of Christ might be shared here, now, and forever.

(Rawle, page 54)

CONNECTING COMMUNALLY WITH THE TOPIC (10 MINUTES)

Welcome the group. Ask group members if they kept their commitments to do one good thing and avoid choosing evil since your last meeting. Encourage those who kept their commitments to share their experiences and to reflect theologically on how these actions honored Jesus.

Transition the group to a time of prayer.

Opening Prayer

Holy Spirit, you lead us into all truth and convict us of sin. Help us learn to better discern right from wrong and to understand that ethics as a follower of Christ involves mature reflection and complex decisions. Guide us in how we think, feel, and act, that in all that we do we bring honor to you. Instill in us strong faith and deep wisdom, that we might always know and do what is pleasing in your sight. In Jesus' name. Amen.

Conversation Starter

Say:

The second chapter in our book explores right, wrong, and holiness. Most of us understand the concepts of right and wrong and as a community we want to acknowledge that right and wrong exist. But we also want to acknowledge that doing what is right is not always easy or simple. Sometimes we are faced with complex ethical situations, and we need God's help in knowing and doing what is right. We must resist evil by standing in the light of Christ, letting him dispel darkness and guide the way. To do so we must commit ourselves to the way of holiness. Today we will discuss how learning from Jesus and relying on him in our daily walk enables us to discern right from wrong and to pursue holiness.

Ask and Discuss:

- Matt Rawle mentions that Spider-Man's commitment to doing what is right is deeply rooted in his failure to stop a criminal who killed his uncle Ben. How does a failure in one situation deepen our resolve to prevent future injustices and to strive for what is right?
- In an earlier Spider-Man comic, a voice tells Peter Parker, "With great power there must also come—great responsibility." What is the relationship between power and status and the responsibility to do what is right?
- How does your faith inform your understanding of right and wrong? What ethical and moral complexities have led you to think more carefully or deeply about your faith?

TAKING A CLOSER LOOK: VIDEO, BOOK, AND SCRIPTURE (40 MINUTES)

Note: This section allows approximately thirty minutes for discussion of the book and Scripture after the video portion concludes. You will not have time to address every discussion question. Select questions in advance you believe will be most helpful for your group and address those questions first. It may help to put a check mark by the questions you want to cover. If time allows, incorporate additional questions.

The Video

Say:

We will continue our time together with a video featuring Matt Rawle. Rawle will talk about the primary themes of our session today:

right, wrong, and holiness. Notice how he explains these themes using pop culture. Make connections to what we have read together in his book. Then, we will discuss both the video and our book together.

Play:

Session 2: Right, Wrong, and Holy (running time is approximately 10 minutes)

Say:

Let's keep what Rawle has said in mind as we take a look at the book and examine these themes in light of our calling to live as disciples of Jesus.

The Book

Chapter two explores our convictions about what is right and wrong. How do we form these convictions? What happens when we are faced with a challenging ethical dilemma? How do we understand Satan? What is the best way to read and apply the Scriptures to everyday situations? What does it mean to live a holy life? These are just a few of the questions that Rawle addresses. Jesus calls us to a life of holiness. What must we do to be found faithful? A tremendous step in the right direction is learning to follow the leading of the Holy Spirit, making a commitment to a mature faith, and embracing the notion that faith is a journey.

Discuss:

- How do we learn to discern right from wrong? How does Christian teaching shape our ethics, and what resources do we draw from in formulating a moral vision?
- What do you think is a wise way of approaching complex ethical dilemmas?
- The author weighs several understandings of the devil, or Satan. Rawle writes, "The devil is a shadow. Shadows

22

are real, but they are only seen when we block the light. So, when we surround ourselves with the light of the Resurrection, in essence, the devil does not exist." What is your understanding of the devil? Offer your reasoning for your understanding at this point in your faith journey.

- Rawle explores the temptation narratives, which tell us how the devil seeks to undermine Jesus. Jesus consistently rejects a good thing for a better thing. He denies the offer of the devil in favor of the will of God. How does Jesus' example instruct us in resisting temptation?

- Rawle cites the example of Rosa Parks as someone who broke a rule in a manner that was just. How did Parks honor the teachings of Jesus? When should rules be broken? Consider reading Acts 4:13-22.

- Rawle states, "The Christian calling is not about being right, and it certainly isn't about constantly being wrong. Our role is to continue God's story, and continuing that story means doing what is holy." What does it mean to do what is holy?

The Scripture

3rd week.

In Advance: Use a commentary or Bible dictionary to help you prepare to discuss the Scripture. Become familiar with the text. Add questions for discussion that emerge from your study in addition to those below.

Read Aloud: Luke 10:25-37

Discuss:

- What are your general observations about this passage?
- Luke 10:29 tells us that the lawyer sought to "justify himself" in asking Jesus, "And who is my neighbor?" What does this suggest concerning the lawyer's motives?

23

- Why does Jesus choose a priest and a Levite as the first two people who pass by the wounded person? What is their significance? Explore with your group how even upstanding religious people can produce good reasons for doing the wrong thing. The priest and Levite may have feared the man was dead and thought touching him would have left them unclean. They may have feared that the bandits were still nearby. They may have also worried this was a trap. They could have been returning home to family and did not want to delay. Try to see and understand how you could do the same thing the priest and Levite chose to do in uncomfortable or dangerous situations.
- The third man Jesus introduces in the story is a Samaritan, who helps the man who was wounded. Do a little research and learn about the relationship between the Jews and the Samaritans. Why does Jesus choose an ethnic and religious outsider as his protagonist?
- Notice the extravagance with which the Samaritan serves the wounded man. What does this suggest about what it means to live a holy life?
- What does this story teach us about right and wrong?
- What does this story teach us about being a neighbor?

Conclude by reflecting on the meaning of this story. Consider how this story illustrates the ease with which we can do wrong and the difficulties that can arise when doing what is right. Also consider the meaning of being a neighbor and how this informs and shapes our understanding of discipleship to Jesus, who calls us to be holy.

Life Application

Say:

As Christians we are called to the way of wisdom in discerning right from wrong. To be wise, we must grow and mature in Christ.

We must be good students of Jesus Christ and develop intimacy with God. We must trust the leading of the Holy Spirit. We should be faithful in worship, good students of the Bible, firmly committed to Christian fellowship, and fervent in prayer. It is our prayer that God would make us holy through participation in the body of Christ.

Matt Rawle writes, "Holiness is our calling as Christians." As a group, define *holiness*. Offer biblical examples. Refer to a Bible dictionary or use a concordance to find places in Scripture where the word *holy* appears.

Once you have a definition, describe a life of holiness. What does a holy life look like? What words are associated with holiness that reflect the goodness and grace of God?

Have each member of the class choose one word that they associate with holiness. *Loving, kind, gentle,* and *joyful* are expressions of holiness. Being loving, kind, gentle, and joyful often lead to doing what is right over what is wrong.

Ask each member of the class to write a prayer to God asking that the word they associate with holiness would be increasingly prominent in their life. Then, send them forth to pray this prayer each day this week. Encourage the class to note if the prayer they pray is answered in specific ways so that they may share those experiences the following week.

SENDING FORTH: EQUIPPED TO SERVE THE WORLD (10 MINUTES)

A Final Thought

Say:

God is holy. In 1 Peter 1:16 the writer instructs followers of Jesus to be holy because God is holy. As we draw near to God we are to reflect God's holiness.

25

Holiness includes knowing right from wrong. But it is deeper. Holiness is more than rule-keeping. It is living life in close communion with God so that God's holiness takes up residence in us. God then works through us to spread love, enact justice, extend compassion, and heal those who are hurting. Let's encourage one another to grow in our faithfulness to Jesus, to trust in him, and to follow his lead.

Closing Prayer

God, you are holy. Make me holy, so that I might know what is right and wrong and consistently choose what is right. Provide the grace that I need to become a person of love, joy, peace, patience, kindness, goodness, and self-control. Make me a person who is a testimony to your beauty, compassion, and mercy. Increase my affection for you. Amen.

Session Three

US, THEM, AND THE BODY OF CHRIST

SESSION OVERVIEW

Lesson Aim

To analyze the human tendency to divide groups into "us" and "them" and examine how Jesus has come to invite all to become part of the body of Christ.

Session Themes

- To reflect carefully on group identity.
- To consider how Christians can be inclusive.
- To realize that a community can consist of unity in diversity.
- To see how true heroes help others discover God's calling on their lives.
- To acknowledge that our heroes can let us down.

- To explore how Christ has brought "us" and "them" together as part of his body.

Hero Focus: Wonder Woman

In each chapter, Matt Rawle cites multiple hero stories to illustrate important biblical and theological concepts. In this chapter, you may want to focus your group on the example of Wonder Woman when exploring the ideas of "us," "them," and the body of Christ. Wonder Woman first appeared in 1941 in *All Star Comics* #8 and was created by William Moulton Marston (aka Charles Moulton) and Harry G. Peter. Wonder Woman's name in her homeland is Princess Diana of Themyscira, Daughter of Hippolyta. She adopts the civilian name of Diana Prince. Diana is the daughter of Queen Hippolyta and the Greek god Zeus. She possesses superhuman powers and is gifted in battle tactics, hunting, and combat, and makes use of advanced technologies including the Lasso of Truth, indestructible bracelets, and a tiara that can be used as a projectile. She is a founding member of the Justice League. Her most notable enemies include Ares, Cheetah, Giganta, Doctor Poison, Doctor Psycho, and Circe. Visit Wikipedia on the Internet and read the entry for Wonder Woman if you would like more information prior to your gathering.

Key Scripture

> *There is no longer Jew or Greek, there is no longer slave or free, there is no longer male and female; for all of you are one in Christ Jesus.*
> *Galatians 3:28*

Theological Focus

If Jesus, when he broke the bread and poured the wine, could gather at the same table both Simon the Zealot (who wanted to overthrow the government) and Matthew the tax collector (who worked for the government), then maybe there's hope for "us" and "them" to become "we."

(Rawle, page 60)

CONNECTING COMMUNALLY WITH THE TOPIC (10 MINUTES)

Welcome the group. Ask group members if they were faithful in praying for God to make them increasingly holy. Did they notice any change? Encourage group members to share their experiences and to reflect theologically on how God changes us to be like Jesus.

Transition the group to a time of prayer.

Opening Prayer

Holy God, you have called us together as your people. In Jesus we have been made one body, united in heart, mind, mission, and service. We are humbly committed to submitting ourselves to one another and to you. You have called us to do justice, love mercy, and walk according to your way. We also ask that you would help us see how you have brought us together as a beautifully diverse community that seeks to honor and glorify the one Lord, Jesus Christ. Our differences are a gift from you. Help us also to love our neighbors, those who are not yet part of your community, so that they might taste and see that you are good. We ask these things in Jesus' name. Amen.

Conversation Starter

Say:

The third chapter in our book explores the ideas of us, them, and the body of Christ. Human beings often tend to create in-groups and out-groups. These divisions can be based on age, race, class, nationality, gender, sexuality, or affinity. At times, these divisions can result in enmity, rivalry, and strife. Jesus came to overcome our divisions and to call forth from humanity a new people, the church. The church is described by Paul in 1 Corinthians 12:12-14 and Ephesians 4:1-16 as the body of Christ. This is a powerful image. Today we will discuss how faith in Jesus brings us into Christ's "one body." It changes how we relate to our neighbors. Being part of the Christian community challenges our understanding of "us" and "them."

Ask and Discuss:

- Matt Rawle asks, "Who are the regional heroes in your city? Whose personality sets the standard for what it means to be a part of your community?" Reflect on your local culture and discuss how yours is unique. How does your regional culture define "us" and "them"?
- What unites the church as the body of Christ? How does the gospel break down barriers between groups of "us" and "them" and give birth to a new "we"?

TAKING A CLOSER LOOK: VIDEO, BOOK, AND SCRIPTURE (40 MINUTES)

Note: This section allows approximately thirty minutes for discussion of the book and Scripture after the video portion concludes. You will not have time to address every discussion question. Select questions in advance you believe will be most helpful for your group and address those questions first. It may help to put a check mark by the questions you want to cover. If time allows, incorporate additional questions.

The Video

Say:

We will continue our time together with a video featuring Matt Rawle. Rawle will talk about the primary themes of our session today: us, them, and the body of Christ. Notice how he explains these themes

30

using pop culture. Make connections to what we have read together in his book. Then, we will discuss both the video and our book together.

Play:

Session 3: Us, Them, and the Body of Christ (running time is approximately 10 minutes)

Say:

Let's keep what Rawle has said in mind as we take a look at the book and examine these themes in light of our calling to live as disciples of Jesus.

The Book

Chapter three explores how Christian people are united together as the body of Christ. Jesus has brought us together. Following Jesus as a disciple changes our relationships with God and our neighbors. Matt Rawle challenges common understandings of the us/them dynamic, reminds us that healthy church communities consist of leaders and followers who mutually serve one another, concedes that many of our heroes make mistakes, and admits that sometimes failed efforts at reaching others for Jesus can teach us something new about the nature of the body of Christ. Rawle wants us to discover God's intention for us: moving us beyond us and them frameworks and toward unity in Jesus Christ.

Discuss:

- What are the "us" and "them" groups that exist in your community? Why do you think these groupings exist? Reflect carefully and draw upon multiple sources of insight. Include theological reasons for division (including sin), as well as historical, psychological, and sociological causes.
- Rawle writes, "If Jesus, when he broke the bread and poured the wine, could gather at the same table both Simon the Zealot (who wanted to overthrow the government) and Matthew the

31

tax collector (who worked for the government), then maybe there's hope for 'us' and 'them' to become 'we.'" Does Jesus *still* bring very different kinds of people together? How?

- Rawle's observation about Simon the Zealot and Matthew the tax collector alludes to Communion, or the Lord's Supper. How does the church's observance of the Lord's Meal serve as both a sign and a foretaste of the kind of unity we have in Christ?

- Rawle observes that Iron Man and Captain America experience conflict and division in *Captain America: Civil War*. Rawle believes that a lack of trust stands at the root of their conflict. How is trust built? How does trust bind a community together? Why is trust important in establishing unity?

- The author explores the ideas of first and second followers. Communities often have leaders, but movements must also have followers. How does the willingness to follow help the body of Christ do good things in the world?

- The author writes that passion, joy, and fruitfulness are solid indicators of calling. Rawle also claims, "Passion is a suffering love." How does passionate service among those in a Christian community serve to foster unity in the body of Christ?

- The author claims, "Heroes reveal to us what it means to be part of a community." Do you agree or disagree? Why?

- Galatians 3:28 says, "There is no longer Jew or Greek, there is no longer slave or free, there is no longer male and female; for all of you are one in Christ Jesus." How does Jesus Christ make us one?

The Scripture

In Advance: Use a commentary or Bible dictionary to help you prepare to discuss the Scripture. Become familiar with the text. Add questions for discussion that emerge from your study in addition to those below.

Read Aloud: John 15:9-17

Discuss:

- What are your general observations about this passage?

- Jesus tells his disciples to abide in his love. What does it mean to abide in the love of Christ? How does the love of Christ unite a community?

- Jesus tells his disciples to "love one another as I have loved you." What does this look like in practice?

- Rawle observes that Jesus "commands [his disciples] to go out and bear fruit that will last—fruit that will last longer than Jesus' early ministry, fruit that will outlive you and me, fruit that will remain until heaven and earth are one." What does it mean to be fruitful as part of the body of Christ?

- How does love help Christian communities to move beyond us/them thinking? How does the abounding of love lead to a wide embrace and a more inclusive "we"?

Conclude by reflecting on your church fellowship. Does your church community abide in the love of Christ? Do you love one another well? Are you sacrificial? Joyful? Obedient to God's commands? Are there people in your church that you would describe as friends of Jesus? Are you bearing fruit? Are you hospitable and welcoming to those who are not part of your community?

Consider and ask if your community is prepared to welcome your neighbors into fellowship with you and with God as part of the body of Christ. If yes, invite others into the "we" of Christ's body. If not, pray that God would help your church be increasingly faithful to God's calling.

Life Application

Say:

As Christians we are called to love all people, serve our neighbors, and announce the good news that in Christ we have been reconciled to God and one another as part of his body. We are to be a community that invites everyone to know that God loved the world so much that Jesus was sent to bring redemption, offering eternal life and forgiveness to those who trust him (John 3:16). All people are invited to partake of God's grace.

As Christ's body we are heralds of that good news message. The gospel is good news for the world.

The gospel also reminds us that we are to lay down our lives in service to our neighbors. But in order to serve our neighbors and show them the love of God we must know them.

In an effort to remove us/them barriers and create the possibility for a stronger "we," take time this week to share a conversation with someone who is different from you. This can be a person in your church community that you do not know well, or an acquaintance from work or your social network. Invite that person to lunch or coffee. Share with your friend or fellow congregant that you are engaged in a study at your church where you are learning the meaning of unity. Say that this week you have been challenged to work for a stronger "we" either in your church fellowship or in your broader community in order to better serve Jesus. Once you set an appointment, pray and ask God to bless your friend and to grant you a fruitful time together.

During your conversation try to listen more than you speak. Ask questions about family, hometown, and life experiences. Also ask your friend where they see us/them divisions in your community and what their opinion is about those divisions. Ask if they see ways to bring about unity, either in the Christian community or in your city. After the conversation concludes take time to jot down your recollections later that day.

Sending Forth: Equipped to Serve the World (10 Minutes)

A Final Thought

Say:

In Ephesians 2:15-18, Paul says Jesus' purpose was to "create in himself one new humanity in place of the two, thus making peace, and . . . reconcile both groups to God in one body through the cross, thus putting to death that hostility through it. So he came and proclaimed peace to you who were far off and peace to those who were near; for through him both of us have access in one Spirit to the Father."

Jesus has overcome us/them divisions to bring about a we: the body of Christ.

In response, we should commit ourselves to one another, abide in Christ, and serve God's purposes. But we should also reach out and invite others to be part of our fellowship, to experience God's love, and to enter into the salvation offered to us through Jesus. Let's encourage one another to grow in faith and to be increasingly fruitful as God's people.

Closing Prayer

Holy Spirit, come and make us one. Enable us to see one another as children of God, as fellow bearers of God's image, and as your beloved in Christ. Make us one as you are one, and send us forth to invite all people into an experience of your grace. In Jesus' name. Amen.

Session Four
HAVE, HAVE-NOT, AND THE KINGDOM OF GOD

SESSION OVERVIEW

Lesson Aim

To recognize the existence of haves and have-nots in society and to challenge those divisions by seeking the kingdom of God.

Session Themes

- To learn to look for the kingdom of God in our midst.
- To understand how life in God's kingdom changes our relationship to our possessions, which includes our wealth.
- To see God's kingdom as a place where human beings stand as equals with one another.
- To realize how having a vision of God's kingdom can lead to incredible acts of service and blessing in the name of Jesus.

- To acknowledge that people are impoverished materially as well as relationally, and that Christians have the opportunity to alleviate loneliness through friendship and presence.
- To explore the practice of thanksgiving.

Hero Focus: Iron Man

In each chapter, Matt Rawle cites multiple hero stories to illustrate important biblical and theological concepts. In this chapter, you may want to focus your group on the example of Iron Man when exploring the concept of haves, have-nots, and the kingdom of God. Iron Man first appeared in 1963 in *Tales of Suspense* #39 and was created by Stan Lee, Larry Lieber, Don Heck, and Jack Kirby. Iron Man is the superhero identity of Tony Stark. Stark is a genius, playboy, and wealthy business magnate who owns Stark Industries. When Stark is kidnapped he sustains a chest injury, and his captors demand that he build a weapon of mass destruction. Instead, Stark builds a super suit powered by a small but immensely powerful reactor. He later perfected his invention, which added super-strength, agility, flight, and other technological advantages to his keen intellect. He then takes on the persona of Iron Man. Iron Man has many enemies, including Doctor Doom, Ultron, Iron Monger, Crimson Dynamo, and the Mandarin. Visit Wikipedia on the Internet and read the entry for Iron Man if you would like more information prior to your gathering.

Key Scripture

I know what it is to have little, and I know what it is to have plenty. In any and all circumstances I have learned the secret of being well-fed and of going hungry, of having plenty and of being in need. I can do all things through him who strengthens me.

Philippians 4:12-13

Theological Focus

The kingdom of God is a place where have and have-not get turned upside down. Unlike the world of Tony Stark, the poor are blessed because the wealthy share. The mournful are comforted, and those with comfort offer lament. . . . God isn't a Robin Hood who steals from the wealthy and gives to the poor, because it's not only money God is calling us to share. God is calling us to share our very self with one another and the world.

(Rawle, page 98)

CONNECTING COMMUNALLY WITH THE TOPIC (10 MINUTES)

Welcome the group. Ask group members if they were able to have a conversation with a person in the congregation or in the community this past week. Ask if they were able to discuss questions concerning us, them, and the body of Christ. Encourage group members to share their experiences and reflect theologically on how God teaches us through interactions with others.

Transition the group to a time of prayer.

Opening Prayer

Dear God—Father, Son, and Holy Spirit—guide our conversation today as we explore what it means to live life in your Kingdom. Help us to see what we have and to offer you thanks, and then strengthen us in using your gifts to bless those who lack. Also help us to see what we lack, and give us grace to trust that you will supply us with what we need. Be present among us today. Let us be quick to listen and slow to speak, sensitive to your leading. Amen.

Conversation Starter

Say:

The fourth chapter in our book explores the ideas of haves, have-nots, and the kingdom of God. In our world, there are those who possess wealth, and those who do not. There are those with power, and there are those who are oppressed. But when Jesus announced the Kingdom he spoke of a series of reversals. In Acts, the early Christians were said to be turning the world upside down (Acts 17:6). Life in God's kingdom calls us to a different way of existence. Christians are called to lend strength to the weary, lift up the downtrodden, and share their resources with those who lack. We do so because we believe this is what Christ has done for us.

Ask and Discuss:

- Matt Rawle asks, "What would it look like for you to share all your possessions with those in need?" Acts 2:44-45 says that the first Christians held everything in common and sold their possessions in order to help anyone who had need. Do you think it is possible for this same kind of generosity to be embraced by the church today? Why or why not?
- How does our vision of God's kingdom shape our everyday choices?

TAKING A CLOSER LOOK: VIDEO, BOOK, AND SCRIPTURE (40 MINUTES)

Note: This section allows approximately thirty minutes for discussion of the book and Scripture after the video portion concludes. You will not have time to address every discussion question. Select questions in advance you believe will be most helpful for your group and address those questions first. It may help to put a check mark by the questions you want to cover. If time allows, incorporate additional questions.

The Video

Say:

We will continue our time together with a video featuring Matt Rawle. Rawle will talk about the primary themes of our session today: the haves, have-nots, and the kingdom of God. Notice how he explains these themes using pop culture. Make connections to what we have read together in his book. Then, we will discuss both the video and our book together.

Play:

Session 4: Have, Have-not, and the Kingdom of God (running time is approximately 10 minutes)

Say:

Let's keep what Rawle has said in mind as we take a look at the book and examine these themes in light of our calling to live as disciples of Jesus.

The Book

Chapter four explores the existence of haves and have-nots in the social order and challenges those categories in light of the kingdom of God. Jesus brings the reign of God, or the kingdom of God. In God's kingdom, those who have share with those who have not. A new kind of economy is born, one in which wealth, power, and influence are stewarded to bring about the flourishing of all. Those in the Kingdom practice thanksgiving for God's many gifts, and are generous with what they have received, having been a beneficiary of the grace and love extended in Jesus Christ. Rawle wants us to see the Kingdom so that we might begin aligning ourselves with the work of God in our midst.

Discuss:

- How do you define "haves" and "have-nots"? The author begins by pointing out disparities between the wealthy and the impoverished. But he also observes those who are relationally impoverished because of their addiction to technology. What are other kinds of "haves" and "have-nots"?
- Rawle claims, "Jesus' ministry reached out to the rich and poor alike, but he vowed that those categories would be turned on their heads in the kingdom of God." How does Jesus bring about a reversal? How does grace change everything?
- Rawle cites a homeless shelter as one place that looks like the Kingdom to him. What places look like the Kingdom to you? Why?
- The author tells a story of a friend who begins a movement that sends thousands of Christmas cards to deployed military servicewomen and servicemen. He says this is an example of someone who embraced Paul's declaration that all things can be done through Christ, the source of our strength. He then mentions that this movement resulted from a vision for God's kingdom and patiently seeking God in prayer. How does connection with Christ change our vision?
- What does the kingdom of God look like? How do you play your part in God's kingdom?
- The author tells a story about a chapel service where many of the students seeking prayer shared that they were lonely. How should Christians respond to the loneliness that is present in our world?
- What practices or disciplines could Christians take up in order to better engage with technology? How would a healthy relationship with technology serve as a witness to our neighbors concerning the power of God?

- The author writes, "Changing our language from blessing to thankfulness is one of the ways we can dissolve the divide between us and our friends." How so? Why is thankfulness important?

The Scripture

In Advance: Use a commentary or Bible dictionary to help you prepare to discuss the Scripture. Become familiar with the text. Add questions for discussion that emerge from your study in addition to those below.

Read Aloud: Philippians 4:4-20

Discuss:

- What are your general observations about this passage?
- In Philippians 4:5 Paul writes, "Let your gentleness be known to all. The Lord is near." How does gentleness toward all people evidence close fellowship with God?
- Read Philippians 4:6-7. What do these verses teach us about prayer?
- How does Paul's connection to Christ change his disposition toward worries? How has this relationship changed his vision? What is the result?
- Read Philippians 4:10-13. How does life in the kingdom of God teach Paul to be content with whatever he has, whether he is in plenty or in want? How does Paul's relationship with Christ sustain him?
- In this passage Paul is thankful for the gifts the church at Philippi has sent through Epaphroditus. How is this an example of provision in God's kingdom? How is this an example of those who "have" meeting his needs of someone who is a "have-not"

- Read Philippians 4:8-9. How do the things we think about shape our disposition toward God's kingdom and work? How does Paul's instruction help reform our thinking so that we might more faithfully live according to God's calling on us in the world?

Conclude by reflecting on God's kingdom. How well does your life reflect the kingdom of God? What about your church? Are you an outpost of God's kingdom, and is that evident in your community? How does your church seek God in prayer? How do you serve others? How do you give witness to the kingdom of God? If you see signs, do not grow weary in doing good. But if you see room for growth, pray for God's direction in meeting real needs in your fellowship and in the broader community.

Life Application

Say:

As followers of Jesus we are called to put the kingdom of God on display. One way we do this is by assessing the resources we have been given by God and then using those resources to bless others.

During our study this week we have acknowledged that in our world there are those who have and those who have not. This week, let's challenge one another to find a way to give up something in order to bless another person.

Let's be creative. Go home and look at your possessions. Perhaps you have shoes that are in good condition or winter coats that could keep another person warm. Donate the good stuff as a blessing. Maybe you have some extra food. Give it away.

Or maybe you don't have much to spare. Perhaps you can fast from one meal this week during a lunch break. Give the money you would have spent otherwise to a person who is hungry, or buy a lunch for someone in need. Alternatively, sell one of your possessions and give away the money to bless another person.

Next week we'll talk about our experiences and reflect on ways we saw God's kingdom at work as we chose to bless others in the name of Jesus.

SENDING FORTH: EQUIPPED TO SERVE THE WORLD (10 MINUTES)

A Final Thought

Say:

In Matthew 4:17, Jesus begins his public ministry and declares, "Repent, for the kingdom of heaven has come near." Jesus announced and enacted the kingdom of God. Through faith in him we become citizens who serve Jesus as Lord and King. Jesus has work for us to do.

Jesus strengthens us for the work, and through him we can do all things. Let's be thankful for his grace. Let's bless others in his name. Let's ask God to give us a vision for his kingdom and pursue it together. Let's invite all who "have-not" to experience what can be theirs in Christ by meeting needs, sharing love, and becoming the people God has called us to be.

Closing Prayer

Lord Jesus, thank you for inviting us into your kingdom family. Help us to join you in turning the world upside down. We give all we have to you and ask you to use us for your Kingdom purposes. Glorify your name in this group of friends, in this church, and in the world. Amen.

Session Five
OLD, NEW, AND COVENANT

SESSION OVERVIEW

Lesson Aim

To identify Jesus as the fulfillment of God's promises to Israel and as one welcoming new people into a covenant relationship with God, and to respond to Jesus with words and actions that testify to God's love.

Session Themes

- To face tensions in our own experiences between established traditions and innovative ways of being the church.
- To see that each of the Gospel writers present Jesus from unique perspectives.

- To understand that the story of God's salvation in the Old Testament is the proper context for understanding the story of Jesus.
- To consider our experiences with Jesus and to learn to tell our faith story.
- To embrace our calling to share our faith in Christ through both words and actions of love.

Hero Focus: Captain America

In each chapter, Matt Rawle cites multiple hero stories to illustrate important biblical and theological concepts. In this chapter you may want to focus your group on the example of Captain America when exploring the ideas of old, new, and covenant. Captain America first appeared in 1941 in *Captain America Comics* #1 and was created by Joe Simon and Jack Kirby. Captain America is the alter ego of Steve Rogers, a frail American military serviceman who received an experimental super-soldier serum that greatly enhanced his strength, endurance, and agility. Captain America was created to assist America in fighting the Germans during World War II, his costume features an American flag motif, and he wields a nearly indestructible shield that he hurls at his foes. He is also the long-time leader of the Avengers. His most notable enemies include Red Skull, Doctor Faustus, Hydra, Baron Zemo, and Flag Smasher. Visit Wikipedia on the Internet and read the entry for Captain America if you would like more information prior to your gathering.

Key Scripture

> *He also told them a parable: "No one tears a piece from a new garment and sews it on an old garment; otherwise the new will be torn, and the piece from the new will not match the old. And no one puts new wine into old wineskins; otherwise the new*

wine will burst the skins and will be spilled, and the
skins will be destroyed. But new wine must be put
into fresh wine skins. And no one after drinking old
wine desires new wine, but says, 'The old is good.'"

Luke 5:36-39

Theological Focus

Jesus was someone who remembered God's story well. His life, suffering, death, and resurrection sparked a revolution that continues to change the world.

(Rawle, page 121)

CONNECTING COMMUNALLY
WITH THE TOPIC (10 MINUTES)

Welcome the group. Ask group members if anyone chose to bless another person in accordance with last week's challenge by giving away something they had, through fasting and subsequent generosity, or by being charitable. Encourage group members to share their experiences and reflect theologically on how God teaches us to see the world differently through participation in God's kingdom.

Transition the group to a time of prayer.

Opening Prayer

Eternal God, Alpha and Omega, the God who was, and is, and is to come, we call upon you to make your presence felt and known among this group of friends. Help us to grow in our knowledge of Jesus during this hour and to see that he came to fulfill the Scriptures and begin a new thing. In him, we are being made a new creation. Change and transform us so that we might become vessels of your love. Amen.

Conversation Starter

Say:

The fifth chapter in our book explores the ideas of old, new, and covenant. The Bible has traditionally been divided into the Old and New Testaments, and the idea of covenant is found throughout Scripture. God's relationship with the people of God is defined by a covenant. A covenant is an agreement between two parties. In the story of Scripture, God promises to relate to humankind in certain ways, and we are expected to relate to God in certain ways. Christians believe that God's promises to Israel have been fulfilled in Jesus and that a new covenant has been inaugurated through the life, death, and resurrection of Jesus. Rawle helps us to see how the Gospel writers explain how Jesus has fulfilled God's promises and begins something new. Rawle also challenges us to live with a heart that is open to God's leading and to see our lives as vessels of God's love.

Ask and Discuss:

- Our chapter this week explores examples of change in congregational life. Has anyone experienced a change in a church you were a part of that resulted in good things, new life, and clear evidence of God at work? What was that experience like? Was the change an easy process?
- Sometimes we face change in congregational life. But we also face personal change. How has God changed you? Has an "old" thing needed to pass away so that you could enter God's "newness" of life?

Taking a Closer Look: Video, Book, and Scripture (40 Minutes)

Note: This section allows approximately thirty minutes for discussion of the book and Scripture after the video portion concludes. You will not have time to address every discussion question. Select questions in advance you believe will be most helpful for your group and address those questions first. It may help to put a check mark by the questions you want to cover. If time allows, incorporate additional questions.

The Video

Say:

We will continue our time together with a video featuring Matt Rawle. Rawle will talk about the primary themes of our session today: the old, the new, and the notion of covenant. Notice how he explains these themes using pop culture. Make connections to what we have read together in his book. Then, we will discuss both the video and our book together.

Play:

Session 5: Old, New, and Covenant (running time is approximately 10 minutes)

Say:

Let's keep what Rawle has said in mind as we take a look at the book and examine these themes in light of our calling to live as disciples of Jesus.

The Book

Chapter five explores the ideas of old, new, and covenant. God's story of salvation is a story of covenant. God has made certain promises to humanity. Yet human beings tend to go their own way—to fall, become broken, and sin. Our brokenness can be personal and individual but also social and systemic. But God is a God of salvation and works to bring about rescue, redemption, and new life. God has offered salvation decisively in Jesus. In this chapter, we want to understand how God is at work in the old and the new, having been bound to the world God has made by the promises God has given in covenant.

49

Discuss:

- Rawle begins the chapter by pointing to Captain America. Captain America's story illustrates the relationship between the old and the new. If you are familiar with the Captain America story as it is portrayed in the recent Marvel movies, how does Captain America navigate the "new" world while retaining and valuing his "old" way of being? How can this example be instructive for the church in a world that is changing?

- Rawle writes, "Jesus isn't so much an innovator as one who remembers God's story and fulfills it." How does Jesus bring about a new future that has continuity with what has been revealed in Israel's story with God?

- The author tells a story of a pastor friend who moved his congregation toward weekly Communion. What did you learn from this story? How was tradition honored? How was it challenged? How did the pastor's approach of honesty create the potential for a more positive outcome? How is this instructive for seeking new avenues for ministry in your congregation?

- Rawle states, "When something new is introduced to a community, the way it's announced is crucial." Do you agree or disagree? Why? What is the best way to introduce something new in a manner that honors God and the community?

- The author explores all four Gospel presentations of Jesus in order to show how each account provides a different perspective and enriches our overall picture of Jesus. How does listening carefully to various experiences with Christ among those who follow him help us obtain a fuller picture of who he is?

- Rawle asks the reader to reflect on his or her experiences of Jesus Christ. Have you ever been asked to tell your faith story? How did you come to know and follow Jesus? What does that relationship mean for your identity?

- The author stresses the importance of actions in conveying what we believe. Words only take us so far. They must be accompanied by love. Rawle writes, "The fifth Gospel is the story you tell through your words and actions." How does your life tell the story of Jesus?

The Scripture

In Advance: Use a commentary or Bible dictionary to help you prepare to discuss the Scripture. Become familiar with the text. Add questions for discussion that emerge from your study in addition to those below.

Read Aloud: Matthew 26:17-30

Discuss:

- What are your general observations about this passage?
- How does the meal Jesus celebrates with his disciples connect to Israel's past? Conduct research on the Passover celebration. It was customary for Jews to celebrate a meal to commemorate and remember how God delivered them from slavery in Egypt. How does this meal remind the disciples that God is a God who saves?
- What new things does Jesus introduce to the meal when he is with the disciples? What did this meal teach the first disciples about the meaning of Jesus' death and resurrection? What does the Lord's Meal teach us?
- The meal Jesus celebrates honors the past, injects meaning into the present, and points toward the future ("I will never drink again of this fruit of the vine until that day I drink it new with you in my Father's kingdom" verse 29). When we celebrate Communion, how do we honor the past, ground ourselves in the present, and look forward to God's future?

- Jesus told his disciples that his blood will be "poured out for many for the forgiveness of sins" (verse 28). How does Jesus' action on the cross free us from our past (the old) and bring us into new life?
- How does the meal Jesus gave to the church help us honor the old and be open to the new? How does it remind us of God's covenant and to always put God's kingdom first?

Conclude by reflecting on God's covenant love. By faith in Jesus we enter into God's covenant family. Our present is redefined. In Christ we have been given a new story; therefore, we have a new history that is also an old history. We also have a future that has been secured for us, one that is filled with hope. Through Jesus we have been written into God's story, which means that God still has new things to bring about in us, in our churches, and in our communities. How are we called to honor our past, celebrate the present, and work toward God's future? What new thing is God doing in us?

Life Application

Say:

This week our group will intentionally reflect on God's covenant and the relationship between the old and new.

God is faithful to his covenant, and thereby God is faithful to his people. We trust that God will be faithful to us because of our trust in Jesus. The stories about Jesus have been faithfully passed along to us by friends, family, or fellow congregants who have learned about Jesus and his ways. They may have passed along their knowledge of Jesus through singing, sound teaching, or through service and example.

Hand each person a note card or a piece of paper. On one side, write "old." This week, think of one thing that is old that helped you enter into a covenant relationship with God. It may have been a pastor, a favorite song or hymn, or an experience that has now become part of the story of your life. Write that down. Think of how you can pass this along to another generation.

Share these ideas with those in leadership. With humility, communicate how these things are meaningful to you, and offer to help in passing these things along to others.

On the other side of your note card or paper write "new." Now, prayerfully think of a person in your congregation or in your community who sees the world differently than you. They may belong to another denomination or generation. They may be someone who does not trust Jesus. Seek out that person. Ask them, "What is one thing that you do not see my church, congregation, or the Christian community doing that you think would help us be better servants of God and all people? What is one 'new' thing we might prayerfully explore as we seek to better serve God and our neighbors? Or is there an 'old' thing we should bring back 'like new' that we have been missing?"

If you are an older person, a younger person might say something about your musical preference in worshiping God. This may create an opportunity for you to learn what music helps younger people worship, and they might also learn why your music is helpful for you in worship. If you speak to someone who is of another religion or of no religion, they may remind you that the church could do a better job of listening or offer a creative idea on how to increase understanding between people with different convictions. There may be a person in your congregation who knows of a need for supporting young mothers, or for helping newlyweds build a strong marriage. Listen and prayerfully seek to discern how God is speaking.

Alternatively, *you* may have felt God calling you or your congregation to do a "new" thing. Write that down.

As a group, share your ideas for ministry with your pastor or the leaders in your congregation. Do so with humility and respect, and ask those in your fellowship to prayerfully consider how God might be leading you to do a new thing.

Consider both the old and new ideas as potential avenues for you to grow in faithfulness to God. God has been faithful to us through covenant. Let's seek to be faithful to God.

SENDING FORTH: EQUIPPED TO SERVE THE WORLD (10 MINUTES)

A Final Thought

Say:

God is constantly leading us and sending us forth into the world to serve. God's salvation is a gift, extended to us. How do we respond? How do we honor God with our words and our deeds? How do we share with others that God has accomplished redemption in Jesus? How do we invite everyone to join in, trust Jesus, and be part of God's future?

Let's live in covenant with God, trusting God's grace, and serve all people with love. Let's invite others to join in, too, for God's goodness, grace, mercy, and forgiveness have been extended to all in Jesus Christ.

Closing Prayer

Lord, you are a God of covenant. Your promises are true and binding, and you are faithful to your people. Help us to serve you today. Help us to show love in your name. Give us the grace we need to reach out to others and invite them to experience life with you. Show us ways to honor what we have received and also to be open to your future. Make us gentle, humble, and joyful. We ask all this in Jesus' name. Amen.

Session Six
LIFE, DEATH, AND RESURRECTION

SESSION OVERVIEW

Lesson Aim

To discuss the importance of the Resurrection for Christian faith and to cite examples of how the Resurrection changes everything.

Session Themes

- To understand how Jesus differs from Superman.
- To contemplate Jesus' comparison of God's kingdom to a mustard seed, a pearl, and a treasure buried in a field.
- To explore the meaning of salvation.
- To consider how discipleship to Jesus involves death and resurrection. Some facets of our life must be put away or left behind in order to take up our cross and follow Christ.

- To realize how the resurrection of Jesus banishes fear and replaces it with joy.
- To see ways Jesus sends us into the world as Resurrection people to heal, bless, serve, and glorify God.

Hero Focus: Superman

In each chapter, Matt Rawle cites multiple hero stories to illustrate important biblical and theological concepts. In this chapter, you may want to focus your group on the example of Superman when exploring the ideas of death, life, and resurrection. Superman first appeared in 1938 in *Action Comics* #1 and was created by high school students Jerry Siegel and Joe Shuster in 1933. Superman's name on his home world of Krypton (which was destroyed) was Kal-El. On Earth, he is named Clark Kent by his adoptive parents, the Kents, who found him as an infant after he crash-landed on their small farm in Kansas. Superman possesses superhuman abilities, including flight, heat vision, x-ray vision, cold breath, and incredible strength, speed, and agility. He is the total package, though he is vulnerable to the element kryptonite, which weakens him. By day, he is a newspaper writer at *The Daily Planet*. His most notable enemies include Lex Luthor, Brainiac, Doomsday, Bizarro, Darkseid, and General Zod. Visit Wikipedia on the Internet and read the entry for Superman if you would like more information prior to your gathering.

Key Scripture

> Jesus said to her, "I am the resurrection and the life. Those who believe in me, even though they die, will live, and everyone who lives and believes in me will never die. Do you believe this?"
>
> John 11:25-26

Theological Focus

Resurrection reveals that death is not the end of the story. Resurrection teaches us that there is nothing to fear. Jesus said that his followers would do even greater works than he. Resurrection is what makes a hero. We are Resurrection people. Go and be a hero!

(Rawle, page 138)

CONNECTING COMMUNALLY WITH THE TOPIC (10 MINUTES)

Welcome the group. Ask group members for their reflections on old, new, and covenant. See what things your group wants to pass on to another generation with regard to their faith. Also consider the ways God may be calling individuals or your fellowship to something new. Remind your group that God is faithful, and encourage them to be faithful to God in response.

Transition the group to a time of prayer.

Opening Prayer

God Almighty, you have the power to raise the dead. You have raised your servant, Jesus. We trust in him, and ask that his power and presence would be manifested among us. Open our hearts and minds to you and your word and enliven our spirits. Guide our conversation today as we explore the meaning of the Resurrection and graciously transform us. In the name of Jesus we pray. Amen.

Conversation Starter

Say:

The sixth chapter in our book explores life, death, and resurrection. The resurrection of Jesus is key for Christian faith. Rawle points toward the Resurrection as a sign of hope as well as an invitation to new life in Christ. This chapter reminds us that death is not the end of the story. Though Jesus "finished" his work on the cross, he was not done. Jesus had more work to do, and we are included in that work through the Resurrection. The world has been changed, and is being changed, because of the resurrection of Jesus Christ. Jesus is the hero of heroes. He has brought us a different and unique salvation. Today we will explore what the Resurrection means for us.

Ask and Discuss:

- Matt Rawle begins this chapter by telling the story of *The Death of Superman*. Did you purchase or read that comic in 1992? How did you react to the idea that the world's greatest hero could die?
- Rawle claims that Jesus is a different kind of hero and that the Resurrection changes everything. How has Jesus been a hero to you? How has the Resurrection changed your life?

TAKING A CLOSER LOOK: VIDEO, BOOK, AND SCRIPTURE (40 MINUTES)

Note: This section allows approximately thirty minutes for discussion of the book and Scripture after the video portion concludes. You will not have time to address every discussion question. Select questions in advance you believe will be most helpful for your group and address those questions first. It may help to put a check mark by the questions you want to cover. If time allows, incorporate additional questions.

The Video

Say:

We will continue our time together with a video featuring Matt Rawle. Rawle will talk about the primary themes of our session today: life, death, and resurrection. Notice how he explains these themes using pop culture. Make connections to what we have read together in his book. Then, we will discuss both the video and our book together.

Play:

Session 6: Life, Death, and Resurrection (running time is approximately 10 minutes)

Say:

Let's keep in mind what Rawle has said as we take a look at the book and examine these themes in light of our calling to live as disciples of Jesus.

The Book

Chapter six explores life, death, and resurrection. In John 11:25-26, Jesus tells Martha, "I am the resurrection and the life. Those who believe in me, even though they die, will live, and everyone who lives and believes in me will never die. Do you believe this?" She responds affirmatively. In Galatians 2:19b-20 Paul writes, "I have been crucified with Christ; and it is no longer I who live, but it is Christ who lives in me. And the life I now live in the flesh I live by faith in the Son of God, who loved me and gave himself for me." Jesus is the resurrection. He was the first to be resurrected from the dead. When we trust him, in a sense our old self is put aside and Christ comes and lives in us. Jesus, our true hero, was raised from the dead. And he raises us up from death to new life. He calls us to be part of his resurrected people, and he leads us as we follow him.

Discuss:

- The author asks, "What in your life needs to be finished so you can enter the kingdom of God?" Rawle mentions alcoholism, workaholism, and shopping addiction as barriers that can stand in our way of following Jesus. What other things can stand in our way of receiving Christ's resurrection life?

- How is Jesus different from Superman?
- What is the meaning of salvation? What does the salvation Jesus offers include for us? How does God save us? What is your understanding? Offer biblical and theological support. What does God save us *for*? What does God save us *from*?
- Rawle writes, "Salvation is not a quick road to ourselves; rather, we let go of ourselves so that we might learn to love God and love one another. As Paul puts it, 'It is no longer I who live, but it is Christ who lives in me' "(Galatians 2:20). What does it mean to die to self and live for God?
- The author states, "When expectation meets the incomprehensible, it leaves us with fear and great joy. Resurrection has changed everything. So, what does that mean?" Rawle offers his interpretation. What would you add? How has the Resurrection changed everything?
- How does the resurrection of Jesus send us forth into the world as heralds of good news and as humble servants of God and neighbor?
- How does the Resurrection dispel our fears? How does the Resurrection bring us joy?
- How is Jesus the ultimate hero?

The Scripture

In Advance: Use a commentary or Bible dictionary to help you prepare to discuss the Scripture. Become familiar with the text. Add questions for discussion that emerge from your study in addition to those below.

Read Aloud: John 20:1-19

60

Discuss:

- What are your general observations about this passage?
- How does the resurrected Jesus surprise his disciples? How do you react to this passage emotionally? What are your feelings toward Jesus? Do you see Jesus as stoic and serious, or playful and inviting? What about the disciples? Do you share in their joy when they recognize that the person on the beach is the Lord? Do you find it funny when Peter jumps out of the boat?
- When the disciples approach Jesus, he serves them breakfast. How does the resurrected Jesus continue to serve us? How does Jesus meet our needs?
- What are the significant elements of Jesus' conversation with Peter? What does this conversation tell you about life, death, and resurrection?
- Peter had a specific calling to teach others about Jesus. Jesus restores Peter three times after Peter had denied Jesus three times. Even though Peter failed, Jesus persists in using him for ministry. Jesus raises Peter up and commands him, "Follow me." How does Jesus continue to use those who fail and fall for his purposes?
- Jesus sent Peter to serve. How does Jesus send us into the world as servants?

Conclude by reflecting on the meaning of Resurrection. How does discipleship to Jesus involve dying to old ways and walking in new ways? How does following Jesus lead to restoration? How does our relationship with the resurrected Jesus send us out to serve? How does Jesus' resurrection give us hope? Consider how in Jesus we have the hope of resurrection. Together, explore how your community gives witness to the reality that in Jesus we have hope.

Life Application

Say:

Read Colossians 3:12-17:

> As God's chosen ones, holy and beloved, clothe
> yourselves with compassion, kindness, humility,
> meekness, and patience. Bear with one another and,
> if anyone has a complaint against another, forgive
> each other; just as the Lord has forgiven you, so you
> also must forgive. Above all, clothe yourselves with
> love, which binds everything together in perfect
> harmony. And let the peace of Christ rule in your
> hearts, to which indeed you were called in the one
> body. And be thankful. Let the word of Christ dwell
> in you richly; teach and admonish one another in
> all wisdom; and with gratitude in your hearts sing
> psalms, hymns, and spiritual songs to God. And
> whatever you do, in word or deed, do everything in
> the name of the Lord Jesus, giving thanks to God the
> Father through him.

Hand out sticky notes or note cards to everyone in your
group. Read this passage aloud twice. The first time, invite
everyone to remain still and listen. During the second reading,
ask each person in the group to listen for one phrase that jumps
out at them. It may be "clothe yourselves with compassion"
or "forgive each other." Paul's instructions in Colossians 3 are
ways we can give witness to the reality that we are Resurrection
people.

Ask group members to share what they wrote down and why.
Then, ask group members to commit to this one thing as a way
to show others how the resurrected life of Jesus has changed
them. If your group is small enough, invite group members to
pray for one another, asking God to strengthen each person and

provide strength for keeping their commitment. If you have a larger group, invite one person to pray for everyone. Send one another forth in the name of Jesus.

SENDING FORTH: EQUIPPED TO SERVE THE WORLD (10 MINUTES)

A Final Thought

Say:

In 1 Corinthians 15, Paul declares that Jesus died for our sins, was buried, and then was raised from the dead in accordance with the Scriptures. Paul also says that Jesus appeared, and people saw him. Paul then writes that because Jesus has been raised we all have the hope of resurrection. He concludes in 1 Corinthians 15:58 saying, "Therefore, my beloved, be steadfast, immovable, always excelling in the work of the Lord, because you know that in the Lord your labor is not in vain."

The Resurrection changes us now as we move from death to life. Jesus has saved us on the cross. But our salvation is being worked out in our daily choices as we follow him. Let's be people of the Resurrection. Let's pray that the world would see Christ at work in us. And let's point the world back to him, giving Jesus all the glory and honor, for he is our hero.

Closing Prayer

Lord Jesus, thank you for conquering sin and death and securing victory for us. We give you thanks for this study and the time we have spent together and with you. We pray that you will help us retain that which will enable us to live faithfully according to your calling, and to continue to grow into mature people of faith. Forgive us when we fail, and empower us for good works. Increase our love for you. Amen.

Made in the USA
Coppell, TX
26 April 2022

77085460R00037